Power Packed Leaders

Are You Ready to Reach Your Destiny?

by

Alicia L Roose Ph.D.

Copyright © 2016 Alicia L. Roose All rights reserved. Including the right to reproduce this book or portions thereof, in any form. No part of this text may be reproduced in any form without the express written permission of the author.

Dedicated to my parents who have always invested in me and supported me through the tough times. Also, to my Pastor and friend who exemplifies leadership to all those round him. Finally, to the one who makes my life worth living. To God who gave me life and gift to lead and write – Thank You.

Chapter

1

On the Right Road

So, you have sorted through the plethora of information on leadership and landed right here. Perhaps you are already in a leadership position and you need to learn some tools to be effective. Maybe, you feel that you are a leader, but those in authority over you seem to look right past you for promotion. Whatever your situation might be, you have started an adventure that will propel you into your destiny. If you take your time and master the following skills, you will find that you will have an influence on those around you.

What makes a Leader? One of the Merriam-Webster definitions of the word Leader is- One who has commanding authority or influence. The question then might be that if a person has a position of authority are they a good leader? The answer is a resounding NO!

Think back to middle school. Of all the kids in your class there always seemed that one or two kids that filtered to the top. They weren't necessarily the smartest kids in the class. You know the guy with the coke bottle thick glasses and plastic pocket protector. Therefore, knowledge does not qualify as a leader. The kids that stood out may not have been the best looking or the hardest working or even the wealthiest kids. So then looks, money, and working yourself to death are not qualifications. So, what was it about them that made kids follow their lead? They could influence the whole class in one direction or another, either in a good way or a bad one.

Leadership is Influence

So, then what *was* that one little thing they had? It was the gift of influence. A little gift that sparks the interest of others to listen and follow. Point blank leadership is being an influence. Those who can influence another empowers them to listen and move in the direction that propels them into their destiny.

You might be thinking do I have that spark? Well, for starters if you didn't you wouldn't be reading this. Secondly, look at the others in your "world". How do they respond to you when you interact with them? If they look to you in crisis or the listen to your advice with a positive outcome, then YES you have it.

Leadership is Responsibility

Now, if you have that spark then you have an amazing responsibility. A responsibility to grab every skill you can learn to add fuel to your fire. In the next few pages, you will find those skills you need to enhance your leadership skills. The responsibility of leadership is not because your name is on your office door or you now have your own business card. If leadership truly is being an influence, how you handle people can make or break your business, your reputation, your relationships, your employees, and your life. Remember those kids back in middle school that led kids down the wrong path? They did not realize their actions impacted so many lives around them. As a leader, you bear the responsibility to influence people. So, you have a chance to influence and build up or you can make choices that negatively impact all that follow you. If a hint of fear swept over you, then that shows you are ready to lead. Take a few minutes and think about how the decisions you have made personally or in business have impacted others' lives. It is said everything you do affects at least 10 other people.

Leadership Styles

Try typing that phrase into a search engine and you will find in excess of 13,6000 sites. It's almost overwhelming. So here is a short list to get you started. There are both positive and negative styles listed. Growing as a leader means identifying your strengths

and your weaknesses.
1. The Charismatic Leader- This style of leader relies on their personality and enthusiasm. You can always spot them because it seems that people flock to hear their ideas. They are flashy, know all the right phrases, and make promises to make changes. While a charismatic leader has a large following, they may lose credibility if they cannot keep their word. This type of leader also tends to wrap their identity in with the group's identity. They also have a tendency to think they are the only one who can lead with results. When the glitter fades the group usually fizzles out.
2. The Servant Leader- Servant Leaders lead strictly by example.

The will not hesitate to roll up their sleeve and work with their team. They will do everything they can to serve those on the team and make sure their needs are met. However, its hard as a leader to see where to go when you are always down on the floor serving. We must always be aware of the needs of those who we are responsible for. However, to truly lead, you must take the helm and steer the ship clear of storms and see the ship safely to port. It's making the hard choices to cut cost in one spot or not go the easy route just to finish a contract.

3. The Mafia Boss Leader- This leader's motto is "it's my way or the highway. They may have a clear direction, but they lead as a

dictator. While structure and organization are important if people are not allowed creativity, the whole vision suffers. Any conflict is met with the idea that "if you don't like the way we do it there's the door". Leadership should foster growth and an exchange of ideas. The most productive people cannot be put in a box. They will become frustrated and leave. The mafia leader uses threats of demotion, pay cuts, having to work longer hours or the opposite promises they don't intend to keep. This creates a hostile environment. An important leadership fact is this: rules without relationship produces rebellion. If you demand obedience without taking the time to build an atmosphere of respect for them then when you make demand those following will complain, become offended, and leave. A simple example is this. If you were to go to a playground and walk up to a kid and command a child to stop throwing rocks. Maybe they might listen, but most often will here "you can't tell me what to do!" On the contrary, if you nephew was throwing rocks and you told him to stop most of the time they will. This is because they know you and what your expectation is. With a mafia leader, the rules are always changing and the leader demands allegiance. By not taking the time to know their followers when an order is given those receiving it rebel or follow with an attitude. This organization has a revolving door of employees who never commit to the purpose of the organization.

4. The Transformational Leader- This is a true visionary who inspires others to follow. They have a clear direction but understand they need the experience of others to get there. The transformation leader is always educating and promoting growth. They are up front leading the way and not hiding behind others. They infect enthusiasm, sell the vision and others flock to them to join. The transformational leader can be wonderful to work with because they foster teamwork. Those following feel a part of some this bigger than they are and will often take ownership. With

ownership, they will gladly sacrifice for the vision by taking payouts, work extra hours, or even invest in the company they work for.

The main drawback of the Transformational Leader can be that they know where they want to go but have no idea how to get there. It would be like wanting to go camping without ever learning all the skills necessary. The don't know how to put up a tent or build a fire, and they don't stop for directions to get to the campsite. A great leader is constantly learning and transforming their lives. They will not only go to a conference but will take they key people with them to make sure they are growing as well. Remember leaders have a responsibility to educate.

Chapter 2

Key Leadership Principles

Principle #1 John Maxwell in his book "The 21 Irrefutable Laws of Leadership" describes a principle called the law of the lid. Put a bunch of fleas in a jar and put a lid to keep them in. Those fleas will jump to the height of the lid in an attempt to get out. However, after a while, you can remove that lid and the fleas will continue only to jump as high as they learned there was a barrier. Yet, because the lid was removed they eventually begin to realize they can jump higher. You may have a small company or team to lead. You see that you are just barely making it, but you want more. If you take the lid off of your limits not only will you grow, others will as well. Non- profits and churches often fall into the trap of not trying a new way. When approached they say "we have always done it this way". While it may have worked five years ago you need to take the lid off. Our technology and economy are always shifting. Do not get pigeonholed in routine. Take the lid off and embrace new ideas.

Principle #2 Ideas always produce consequences. If you take anything away from this eBook learn this principle. **Everything** you do in life has either a positive or negative outcome. For instance, if you as a leader decide to take on a partner who you think will better your company. You integrate them into your business and give them assess to your staff. As a month goes by you begin to notice that your new partner has been making business deals, but not honestly representing your company. He makes promises to your vendors with no intention of delivering. Your partner has an integrity problem. Even if you remove him the damage is catastrophic. Your vendor no longer wants to deal with your company. Your image has been damaged and your profits slip away. That idea of taking on a partner may have been a much need thing for you. It looked good, but the consequences reached far beyond what the benefits could have.

If you are a startup project, or if you just stepped into a position hold on to this principle. If your idea that you are going to be small, then you plan small.

However, if you take off that lid and think big then you will be. You may have only 5 employees. Think big and plan to have 50. Even if that seems impossible you must start the process. Get a solid training program so you can train 50 people even if you only need to train 3 right now. What you do when you are beginning can be the solid bedrock you stand on when you are expanding. Ideas always produce consequences

Principle #3 Lead where you are. Perhaps you are in charge of only a division or team. It is only a part of the company and you have no title nor do you have any authority. Can you lead from the middle? Yes, you can. If you truly have leadership qualities, you can pull out the best in those around you. If you are just a "climber" wanting to rise to the top or looking for a title you will be in trouble. Those around you can see what you are made of quickly. Being genuine and looking out for the interest of your company as well as those around you will show you can handle a position.

Have you ever been a part of a team to accomplish a project or to brainstorm? Almost, immediately the leaders rise to the front. Now there can be two leaders. They can either work together or they cause a fight for power. Nothing with two heads can be healthy. People discern who is the person who will best represent them. If you take the responsibility to learn all you can to lead where you are, you will be successful.

Principle #4 Work yourself out of a job. You might be thinking "that's absolutely nuts, I am the boss and no one is going to take my job." There is a law of nature that everything reproduces. If you do not mentor one other person to do what you do, then when your gone everything dies with you.

For example, a man started a non-profit to teach young men in the community how to build houses. This man pulls troubled kids together and the go into the run down, abandon houses and renovate them. The then sell those home at such a low-cost family can own a home for the first time. Then one day that man is in an accident and no longer able to work. He never took the time to show anyone how to do everything that he did not make his vision a success. Others can try to fill his shoes and keep things going and struggle. Within a year, the project dissolves. If that man had mentored two or three other young men to do his job, then most likely the project would have gone on for years to come. As a leader do not be threatened by others around you. If you have the idea that if you train someone to do what you do you will lose your position you are in a danger zone. If you hold of too tight to something, it gets chokes out. Learn to let go and take the lid off. Take the responsibility to learn new leadership skills. Invest in those around you. Look for the best qualities in your teammates and encourage them that they can grow and achieve. If you do these thing people will naturally follow you. If you train the next person to replace you then you leave stepping stones for others to land on. That is the sign of a true leader.

Chapter

3

Effective Communication

Learning to effectively communicate is vital. In this chapter you will learn three things:

- How to empower others to hear you.
- How to ensure a person hears you and successfully completes the job.
- Learn how people process what you say

Have you ever had the experience of talking to someone and you know they are not listening? It can be irritating for the one doing the talking. On the other hand, if someone is talking to you and you can't connect or process what they are saying the frustration for the listener is the same. HOW you talk to people can help them engage and buy into what you are saying.

Communication Key #1 Empowering Your Audience

How do you empower someone to listen to you? It is really a matter of courtesy. In our high-tech society, we are in danger of losing this important art. If you really listen and not look at your watch, let your mind wonder what to make for dinner, calculate the time you have left to get to your next meeting, or think about the good-looking person three tables over; then you empower them. In our fast-passed world, we are more apt to text, email, skype, or tweet then to actually take the time to listen to someone. However, if you take time to listen you will find you will receive something in return. As you listen, you gain permission for them to listen to you. Now you may say, 'you have no idea how my secretary loves to talk. I mean, if I actually had to listen to every word she says I would never get anything done." While there are people who seem to love to hear themselves talk. perhaps it is because they feel they are the only ones listening.

Communication Key #2 Actions Speak Louder than Words

There is an inborn need to be heard.

The art of communication goes beyond verbal sound. Another important factor is body language. If you are closed up and standing with your arms folded, then those listening to you will hear your words as threatening. Here are a few quick tips to score some listening points.

- Maintain eye contact
- Stay focused by asking questions or making notes to bring something back up later.
- Keep an open body posture
- Learn forward slightly
- Watch your facial expressions.

How a person perceives your body language can either draw them in or shut them off. There is a great deal of information on this subject. Remember great leaders are those that learn how to improve their effectiveness.

Communication Key #3 Know the Flow

O.K. so you have done your job listening. You have made sure to check how you are presenting yourself now it's time to start talking. There is a simple way to make sure that your listener is grasping what you are saying. A great rule to remember is to:

1. Say what you're going to say
2. Say it plainly
3. Say what you just said.

That seems way to easy, doesn't it? However, if you do this when giving directions you can ensure you will be heard. When we process information, we do it in steps. Point "A" to step "B" and so forth. Some people are extremely quick and grasp the information and go. Yet others, it takes a few minutes. As leaders, it is important to make sure those listening is processing through our directions. Here is a great example of a conversation with a new employee that needs to learn to use the copy machine.

You: "Hi Mike! I see that you need to learn to use the copy machine. So here is what needs to happen. Every employee has a copy machine code. Do you have yours with you?'

Mike: "Yes it 25425"

You: "Great! So, Mike, this is how it works. First, enter your code on this keypad. Second, pick the size and number of copies, and push the green button. Got it?"

Mike: "Sure, sounds easy."

You: "It can take a few minutes. Why

don't you talk me through the steps?"

Mike: "Well I think you said that first I need to punch my code in, but I'm not sure if this is where I enter it."

You: That's right! Enter your code, pick your size and number of copies then push the green button. Let's see you give it a try.

Mike completes the task.

You: "Fantastic Mike. That wasn't so bad, was it? Just remember your three steps: enter your code, make your selections, and push green for go. If you have any questions give me a call. Thanks, Mike you did great."

Let's notice a few things. You walked Mike through the steps being careful to explain everything. Yet Mike had a problem remembering all the steps. He listened but didn't process everything. Always be careful not to rush a person which causes frustration. It may take someone to see one time all the steps, but others need to go through the steps two or three times. We all learn at different speeds. Sometimes we as leaders can give directions quickly because *we* are on a schedule assuming when you return it will be done correctly. Always remember this: Inspect what you expect.

If you leave a team, a group or a new employee with a task go back two times. First to check to ensure they have grasped the task and the second time inspect to see if it was done correctly. A good leader can give good directions. However, a great leader follows through and makes it a point to follow up on the directions they gave.

This can be a quick as a phone call, an email, or a text. It could be an easy as a walk back through the office to touch base with everyone. It is vital that when you lead others know that you care enough to take the time for them.

Communication Key #4 The Power of Positives

Florence Littauer is a well know American public speaker has a message called "The Silver Box with a Bow on Top". She was asked to speak to some children about the meaning of edifying words. She was told by one girl 'it means to 'build up'. When she asked how you could build up, one boy said 'it's like when you're playing with building blocks; you shouldn't knock down other people's building blocks'. Florence was able to get the children to explain to her that words could be like

this. They could knock down other people's building blocks, but they should not do this, instead, they should build up by using good words.
As leaders, we have the power to build up or tear down. We have to be cognizant of it. What it shouldn't matter is you are in a hurry or in a bad mood. Be aware of how you speak and the way to say it. If you can master the power of positives people will follow you. Even when bringing correction always end by saying something positive. Face it, some people just get on our nerves and when they walk into the business meeting we want to avoid talking to them. They can single-handedly ruin your whole day. What would happen if you took the lead and made them feel positive? The only thing positive you can see about them is that they can tie their shoes. Then, by all means, say it.

Chapter

4

Leadership in Practice

Great leaders choose their leadership styles like a golfer chooses a club: with a clear understanding of the end goal and the best tool for the job. Taking a team from ordinary to extraordinary means understanding

and embracing the difference between management and leadership.
According to writer and consultant Peter Drucker, "Management is doing things right; leadership is doing the right things."

Manager and *leader* are two completely different roles, although we often use the terms interchangeably. Managers are facilitators of their team members' success. They ensure that their people have everything they need to be productive and successful; that they're well trained, happy and have minimal roadblocks in their path; that they're being groomed for the next stage; that they are recognized for great performance and coached through their challenges.

However, a leader can be anyone on the team who has a particular talent, who is creatively thinking out of the box and has a great idea, who has experience in a certain aspect of the business or project that can prove useful to the manager and the team. A leader leads based on strengths, not titles.

The best managers consistently allow different leaders to emerge and inspire their teammates (and themselves!) to the next level.

When you're dealing with ongoing challenges and changes, and you're in uncharted territory with no means of knowing what comes next, no one can be expected to have all the answers or rule the team with an iron fist based solely on the title on their business card. It just doesn't work for day-today operations. Sometimes a project is a long series of obstacles and opportunities coming at you at high speed, and you need every ounce of your collective hearts and minds and skill sets to get through it.

This is why the military style of top-down leadership is never effective in the fast-paced world of adventure racing or, for that matter, our daily lives (which is really one big, long adventure, hopefully!). I truly believe in Tom Peters' observation that the best leaders don't create followers; they create more leaders. When we share leadership, we're all a heck of a lot smarter, more nimble and more capable in the long run, especially when that long run is fraught with unknown and unforeseen challenges.

CHANGE LEADERSHIP STYLES

Not only do the greatest teammates allow different leaders to consistently emerge based on their strengths, but also, they realize that leadership can and should be situational, depending on the needs of the team. Sometimes a teammate needs a warm hug. Sometimes the team needs a visionary, a new style of coaching, someone to lead the way or even, on occasion, a kick in the bike shorts. For that reason, great leaders choose their leadership style like a golfer chooses his or her club, with a calculated analysis of the matter at hand, the end goal and the best tool for the job.

My favorite study on the subject of kinetic leadership is Daniel Goleman's *Leadership That Gets Results*, a landmark 2000 *Harvard*

Business Review study. Goleman and his team completed a three-year study with over 3,000 middle-level managers. Their goal was to uncover specific leadership behaviors and determine their effect on the corporate climate and each leadership style's effect on bottom-line profitability.

The research discovered that a manager's leadership style was responsible for 30% of the company's bottom-line profitability! That's far too much to ignore. Imagine how much money and effort a company spends on new processes, efficiencies, and cost-cutting methods in an effort to add even one percent to bottom-line profitability and compare that to simply inspiring managers to be more kinetic with their leadership styles. It's a no-brainer.

Here are the six leadership styles Goleman uncovered among the managers he studied, as well as a brief analysis of the effects of each style on the corporate climate:

1. **The pacesetting leader** expects and models excellence and self-direction. If this style were summed up in one phrase, it would be "Do as I do, now." The pacesetting style works best when the team is already motivated and skilled, and the leader needs quick results. Used extensively, however, this style can overwhelm team members and squelch innovation.
2. **The authoritative leader** mobilizes the team

toward a common vision and focuses on end goals, leaving the means up to each individual. If this style were summed up in one phrase, it would be "Come with me." The authoritative style works best when the team needs a new vision because circumstances have changed, or when explicit guidance is not required. Authoritative leaders inspire an entrepreneurial spirit and vibrant enthusiasm for the mission. It is not the best fit when the leader is working with a team of experts who know more than him or her.

3. **The affiliative leader** works to create emotional bonds that bring a feeling of bonding and belonging to the organization. If this style were summed up in one phrase, it would be "People

come first." The affiliative style works best in times of stress, when teammates need to heal from a trauma, or when the team needs to rebuild trust. This style should not be used exclusively, because a sole reliance on praise and nurturing can foster mediocre performance and a lack of direction.

4. **The coaching leader** develops people for the future. If this style were summed up in one phrase, it would be "Try this." The coaching style works best when the leader wants to help teammates build lasting personal strengths that make them more successful overall. It is least effective when teammates are defiant and unwilling to change or learn, or if the leader lacks proficiency.

5. **The coercive leader** demands immediate compliance. If this style were summed up in one phrase, it would be "Do what I tell you." The coercive style is most effective in times of crisis, such as in a company turnaround or a takeover attempt, or during an actual emergency like a tornado or a fire. This style can also help control a problem teammate when everything else has failed. However, it should be avoided in almost every other case because it can alienate people and stifle flexibility and inventiveness.
6. **The democratic leader** builds consensus through participation. If this style were summed up in one phrase, it would be "What do you think?"

The democratic style is most effective when the leader needs the team to buy into or have ownership of a decision, plan, or goal, or if he or she is uncertain and needs fresh ideas from qualified teammates. It is not the best choice in an emergency situation, when time is of the essence for another reason or when teammates are not informed enough to offer sufficient guidance to the leader.

Bottom line? If you take two cups of authoritative leadership, one cup of democratic, coaching, and affiliative leadership, and a dash of pacesetting and coercive leadership "to taste," and you lead based on need in a way that elevates and inspires your team, you've got an excellent recipe for long-term leadership success with every team in your life.

Chapter 6

The Servant Leader

The servant-leader is servant first. It begins with the natural feeling that one wants to serve. Then conscious choice brings one to aspire to lead. The best test is: do those served grow as persons; do they, while being served, become healthier, wiser, freer, more autonomous, more likely themselves to become servants? —Robert K. Greenleaf

The mightiest of rivers are first fed by many small trickles of water, and an apt way of conveying my belief that the growing number of individuals and organizations practicing servant-leadership has increased from a trickle to a river. Servant-leadership is also an expanding river, and one which carries with it a deep current of meaning and passion. The servant-leader concept continues to grow in its influence and impact. In many ways, it can truly be said that the times are only now beginning to catch up with Robert Greenleaf's visionary call to servant-leadership. The idea of servant-leadership, now in its fourth decade as a concept bearing that name, continues to create a quiet revolution in workplaces around the world. In countless for-profit and not-for-profit organizations today we are seeing traditional, autocratic, and hierarchical modes of leadership yielding to a different way of working—one based on teamwork and community, one that seeks to involve others in decision making, one strongly based in ethical and caring behavior, and one that is attempting to enhance the personal growth of workers while improving the caring and quality of our many institutions. This emerging approach to leadership and service is called servant-leadership.

The words servant and leader are usually thought of as being opposites. When two opposites are brought together in a creative and meaningful way, a paradox emerges. And so, the words servant and leader have been brought together to create the paradoxical idea of servant-leadership. The basic idea of servant leadership is both logical and intuitive. Since the time of the industrial revolution, managers have tended to view people as objects; institutions have considered workers as cogs within a machine. In the past few decades we have witnessed a shift in that long-held view. Standard practices are rapidly shifting toward the ideas put forward by Robert Greenleaf, Stephen Covey, Peter Senge, Max DePree, Margaret Wheatley, Ken Blanchard, and many others who suggest that there is a better way to lead and manage our organizations.

The following characteristics are central to the development of servant-leaders:

1. Listening: Leaders have traditionally been valued for their communication and decision-making skills. While these are also important skills for the servant-leader, they need to be reinforced by a deep commitment to listening intently to others. The servant-leader seeks to identify the will of a group and helps clarify that will. He or she seeks to listen receptively to what is being said (and not said!). Listening also encompasses getting in touch with one's own inner voice and seeking to understand what one's body, spirit, and mind are communicating. Listening, unique spirits. One assumes the good intentions of co-workers and does not reject them as people, even while refusing to accept their behavior or performance. The most successful servant-leaders coupled with regular periods of reflection, is essential to the growth of the servant-leader.

2. Empathy: The servant-leader strives to understand and empathize with others. People need to be accepted and recognized for their special and are those who have become skilled empathetic listeners.

3. Healing: Learning to heal is a powerful force for transformation and integration. One of the great strengths of servant-leadership is the potential for healing one's self and others. Many people have broken spirits and have suffered from a variety of emotional hurts. Although this is a part of being human, servant leaders recognize that they have an opportunity to "help make whole" those with whom they come in contact.

4. Awareness: General awareness, and especially self-awareness, strengthens the servant-leader. Making a commitment to foster

awareness can be scary—you never know what you may discover. Awareness also aids one in understanding issues involving ethics and values. It lends itself to being able to view most situations from a more integrated, holistic position.

5. Persuasion: Another characteristic of servant-leaders is a primary reliance on persuasion, rather than using one's positional authority, in making decisions within an organization. The servant-leader seeks to convince others, rather than coerce compliance. This particular element offers one of the clearest distinctions between the traditional authoritarian model and that of servant-leadership. The servant-leader is effective at building consensus within groups.

6. Conceptualization: Servant-

leaders seek to nurture their abilities to "dream great dreams." The ability to look at a problem (or an organization) from a conceptualizing perspective means that one must think beyond day-to-day realities. For many managers this is a characteristic that requires discipline and practice. The traditional manager is focused on the need to achieve short-term operational goals. The manager who wishes to also be a servant-leader must stretch his or her thinking to encompass broader based conceptual thinking. Within organizations, conceptualization is also the proper role of boards of trustees or directors. Unfortunately, boards can sometimes become involved in the day-today operations 4 The Understanding and Practice of Servant-Leadership - Spears (something that should always be discouraged!) and fail to provide the visionary concept for an institution.

Trustees need to be mostly conceptual in their orientation, staffs need to be mostly operational in their perspective, and the most effective CEOs and leaders probably need to develop both perspectives. Servant-leaders are called to seek a delicate balance between conceptual thinking and a day-to-day focused approach.

7. Foresight: Closely related to conceptualization, the ability to foresee the likely outcome of a situation is hard to define, but easy to identify. One knows it when one sees it. Foresight is a characteristic that enables the servant-leader to understand the lessons from the past, the realities of the present, and the likely consequence of a decision for the future. It is also deeply rooted within the intuitive mind. As such, one can conjecture that foresight is the one servant-leader characteristic with which

one may be born. All other characteristics can be consciously developed. There hasn't been a great deal written on foresight. It remains a largely unexplored area in leadership studies, but one most deserving of careful attention.

8. Stewardship: Peter Block (author of Stewardship and The Empowered Manager) has defined stewardship as "holding something in trust for another. "Robert Greenleaf's view of all institutions was one in which CEOs, staffs, and trustees all played significant roles in holding their institutions in trust for the greater good of society. Servant-leadership, like stewardship, assumes first and foremost a commitment to serving the needs of others. It also emphasizes the use of openness and persuasion rather than control.

9. Commitment to the growth of people: Servant-leaders believe that people have an intrinsic value beyond their tangible contributions as workers. As such, the servant-leader is deeply committed to the growth of each and every individual within his or her institution. The servant-leader recognizes the tremendous responsibility to do everything within his or her power to nurture the personal, professional, and spiritual growth of employees. In practice, this can include (but is not limited to) concrete actions such as making available funds for personal and professional development, taking a personal interest in the ideas and suggestions from everyone, encouraging worker involvement in decision making, and actively assisting laid-off workers to find other employment.

10. Building community: The servant-leader senses that much has been lost in recent human history as a result of the shift from local communities to large institutions as the primary shaper of human lives. This awareness causes the servant-leader to seek to identify some means for building community among those who work within a given institution. Servant-leadership suggests that true community can be created among those who work in businesses and other institutions.

These ten characteristics of servant-leadership are by no means exhaustive. However, I believe that the ones listed serve to communicate the power and promise that this concept offers to those who are open to its invitation and challenge.

Chapter 7

The Heart of the Matter

So far in this book I have given skills to help you succeed in leadership. However, to be a good leader we must look inward to the type of person we really are on the inside. I have seen CEOs of a big company walk all over people, use people for his gain, and live in a way that make those around him feel demeaned. That is not the goal of rising to the top. On the contrary, I have known CEOs of corporations that people will take a pay cut to come work for because they make people feel like they can accomplish their dream. These leaders are not ashamed to work in the community or serve at the local soup kitchen. Instead of gaining wealth they are always looking for ways to help others. What kind of leader do you want to be known as?

    As I have mentioned leadership is influence. In this chapter we are going to do a scary thing and set aside the topic of leadership and take up the mirror of looking inward. What kind of person are you really? I mean when it's just you and there is no one to impress. Are you confident or are you really insecure trying to act confident? Are you assertive when inside your really shaking in your shoes all the time? When the rubber meets the road what's really on the inside of you will come out. You character will be seen by those around you. I teach youth that you are like a tube of toothpaste when you are under pressure what is really on the inside will come out. That's your true character. Ouch.

In leadership character is everything. The core of the matter is what's going on in your heart. What is happening in your heart impacts your family and everyone around you. In your relationships you can have a super power. Yes, I really mean it. You can have a superpower that propels you forward in every area of your life. That power is forgiveness. You may balk and say but you don't know how they stole my promotion or how they hurt me. Let it go. Harboring anything in your heart will only hurt yourself. This is an excerpt from my book *"Learning to Live Set Free"*.

Explosive Forgiveness

Forgiveness is one of the most dynamic powers you could ever possess. It is, however, hard to learn to walk in because our emotions are involved. I want to give you an illustration of what it means to be alive.

There once were two porcupines sleeping close to each other. As they slept their long sharp quills lay tight to their bodies. Tranquility and peace reigned until a loud sound suddenly woke the first porcupine. Startled, his quills stood on end poking the poor sleeping porcupine next to him. The second porcupine hurt and angry shot his quills at the first porcupine. Both wounded by the other, walked away angry determined not to get close again.

Which porcupine do you relate to the most? Somewhere in your life, you have been one or the other or maybe both porcupines. The key is what will you do about it? To forgive the one that hurt you for some seems impossible. I can hear someone say, "You just don't know what they did to me!". Wounds of the heart do not heal easily. The hurts of a child now grown are like a wound that has been left to fester and become infected. The only way to heal is to get to the heart of the matter – forgiveness.

In Mathew chapter 6 Jesus was teaching about prayer. He gives us a powerful pattern to prayer that we commonly call "The Lord's Prayer". Right in the heart of the prayer he says

Matthew 6:12 Amplified Bible (AMP) 'And forgive us our debts, as we have forgiven our debtors [letting go of both the wrong and the resentment].

Perhaps you have heard of Isaac Newton's Third Law- For every action there is an equal or opposite reaction. That Law that God showed Isaac Newton can be applied here. If you want the forgiveness of God, you must also forgive those in your life.

Is it true that if I walk in unforgiveness God will not forgive me? Let's look at it like this. Unforgiveness is like cancer of the soul. It eats away at you. Consider this story.

There once was a man who went into a local shoe store to buy a pair of shoes. The sales clerk was having a bad day and didn't greet the man. The man found a pair of shoes he wished to purchase, but he didn't see his size on the shelf. He took the shoes to the clerk who was busy reading a newspaper and asked if they had his size. The clerk replied sharply that if his size wasn't on the shelf they didn't have it and went back to reading the paper. Offended and angry the man quickly left the shop vowing never to come back again. Not only did he not go back for years he told everyone he knew not to visit that establishment even though many told him that store had the best shoes in town. One day, many years later, his shoes were desperately wearing out. He went to every store in town and could not find what he needed. Walking by "THAT" shoe store he saw the shoes he needed in the window display. Not only that but they were his exact size. Muttering to himself that he must be crazy he entered the store and was greeted by two sales people who helped him find the shoes, insisted he try them on to be sure he would be happy with them and gave him a 10% discount. Nowhere in the store was the clerk he experienced long ago.

Can you see how unforgiveness became a cancer to his soul? His bitterness could have infected others over the years costing the store owner in sales. Unforgiveness and Bitterness are good friends and usually hang out together. In fact, if you let them in your life for two long doctors have proven you may have health risks.
So then to understand the explosiveness of forgiveness perhaps you need to understand the difference between a

chicken and an eagle.

Chickens and Eagles.
 The difference between chicken and eagles is their focus. Chickens, for the most part, are downward lookers. They pick at the ground looking for grubs or bugs, they lay their eggs in nests on the ground or in a coup. They can fly but usually only enough to get up in the air and then only go a short distance before returning to the ground. Those who walk with unforgiveness OR who do not understand the radical forgiveness of God are focusing low. It's hard when someone you loved left you, someone stole from you or you experienced loss for no good reason. Life can be brutal. Just like those porcupines, those offences can stick deep in our hearts. There is one who understands. His name is Jesus.

Can you imagine being in heaven and being part of the Creator with all power and knowledge? How amazing that would be. So, Adam and Eve are created and placed in the garden for a relationship and all of the creation was at their disposal EXCEPT one tree. Sure, enough Satan himself slithers into the garden still determined to exalt himself above God. He whispers to Adam and Eve. They fall into his evil plan and sin enters the world. Adam and Eve are removed from the garden and Satan thinks that he has a victory. He knows sin cannot be in the presence of a Holy God and he has cut off God's prize creation from Him. A huge gulf stood between God and man. Satan believes he has won, but little did He count on love. Jesus stands and tells God the Father that He will be the bridge. So, the Father begins setting the stage. Down through time, He weaved a scarlet thread until the time was right. Jesus does something magnificent. He leaves His heavenly thrown where He never had need of anything to step through the portal of time into the frail frame of an infant. He surrendered the arms of heaven to be placed in the arms of his mother Mary. He experienced need, hunger, longing for love and acceptance. He had to learn to control emotions, appetites, desire and urges. He made friends, had friends leave him, he even had them betray him. He experienced stress in the garden of Gethsemane so much that He sweat drops of blood. When he was beaten and made to carry the cross that was ment for us, He stumbled and fell under the weight too weak to go on. Another man was there to carry it for Him. Yet the Bible says no man took His life. When the Roman soldier commanded him to lay down on the cross Jesus willingly stretched out His hands to be nailed. Nailed to a tree He created, suspended by nails whose elements He held together by His word, hung under a sky He spoke into existence. All because He loved you. All to forgive you.

He understands the pain involved in forgiving and receiving forgiveness. He understands right where your heart is at, but you can be like a chicken and have low thinking and chew on bitterness, hurt, anger, resentment and never fly higher than the walls you've built, or you can change.

Really think this through- Who are you hurting walking in unforgiveness, building up walls, keeping others away or being bitter or angry?

Eagle

Eagles soar high on the winds far above all the trivial. They fly free and feed on only that which is alive. When Eagles mate they mate for life. When they are in trouble or are under attack an eagle will fly straight into the suns brilliance to blind its prey. If an eagle eats something poisoned it doesn't hold on to it. It will fly to a high place and lay with its wings spread out on the rocks to allow the Sun to burn all the poison out of it.

Isa 40:30-31 **30**Even youths will become weak and tired, and young men will fall in exhaustion.
31But those who trust in the LORD will find new strength. They will soar high on wings like eagles.
They will run and not grow weary. They will walk and not faint.

Jesus asks us to forgive our debtors just as He forgives us. What if the person you need to forgive is yourself?
Who is harder for you to forgive others or yourself?

Some people can let themselves off the hook relatively quickly but for some of us letting ourselves off the hook is like trying to climb Mount Everest. Sometimes we have been made to do things through abuse or we chose to do somethings on our own that we are ashamed off. Regardless of the cause, if you had to do things then you can choose to look at them and ask God for forgiveness. Then you must remind yourself that if God can forgive you and He loves you so much then you can find a way to let go as well. That's really what forgiving yourself is - Letting Go. Just a note- just because you forgave that person does not mean you should put yourself back into that position or put an approval on their actions.

Most of us know about the 10 commandments found in Gen. 20. These Commandments were set by God as a moral compass to govern one's life by. The Jewish Law was given to show that no matter how hard man tried they could never be Holy or sinless. We needed a Savior. Jesus in
Mark 12:28-31 was asked which is the greatest commandment to live by.

28And one of the scribes came and having heard them reasoning together, and perceiving that he had answered them well, asked him, which is the first commandment of all?

29 And Jesus answered him, the first of all the commandments is, Hear, O Israel; The Lord our God is one Lord:

30 And you shall love the Lord your God with all your heart, and with all your soul, and with all your mind, and with all your strength: this is the first commandment.

31 And the second is like, namely this, you shall love your neighbor as yourself. There is no other commandment greater than these.

We seem to be able to do the first one easily. The second poses a problem for some. You Shall love your neighbor as yourself. What if you don't love yourself? What if you have a chicken's view.

Another way forgiveness is explosive is through freedom. When you learn to forgive others and how easy it is to walk with that Eagle, view joy will begin to return to your life. Sometimes you might have to go to a person and ask them to forgive you for the wrongs you have done. They may not even remember, or they may even say no, BUT you took the liberating steps. When we carry all these wounds, bitterness, anger, resentments or shame it's like carrying a backpack full of rocks around. What a burden to carry.

Joyce Meyers – You can be pitiful, or you can be powerful, but you can't be both.

Activity One- It's not just enough to say words. To remove something from our long-term memory or our emotions we feel deeply we must also act. For some, this will be a piece of cake but for others, this might be more difficult.

On a piece of the paper list those you need to forgive. Include your self. You don't need to write a paragraph retelling yourself all they did. Just write their name. Then one by one asks God to forgive them and talk to God about how it. Listen for Him to speak to you. When you think you've resolved that name cross it off and move to the next. Allow the tears to flow if you need to and let God Cleans your heart. When it comes to your name – take your time. When you are finished fold the paper and tearing up and throw it away. You might think this is unimportant, but phycologist tells us the act of seeing the name crossed off and then tearing up the paper bring a closure. There is an actual chemical reaction in your brain and endorphins are released.

Activity Two – Begin to journal as you go through this course. It's important because you can see how far God had brought you. By documenting how you felt, what you learned, what you let go of, who you forgave, what decisions you made you shut the door in the devil's face. When he comes to try to remind you of who you used to be or bring up that person you forgave you can remind yourself and him that it's under the blood of Jesus.

Confidence Key

Along with forgiveness the power of inner confidence separates average leaders from great leaders. All leaders are expected to make tough decisions.

It's not easy being at the top. However leaders without confidence stand on shaky ground and lose the respect of the people they are leading. People do not trust or want to follow leaders who lack confidence. On the other hand, leaders with self-confidence garner the respect of the people they are leading because of their decisiveness.

Are you a confident leader? Here are five awesome traits that you can use as a gauge.

1. Communication

Effective communication is one of the keys to being a confident leader. Communicating key concepts in an easy to understand way builds those around you. Confident leaders do not have to feed their egos by speaking down to those they are leading. They speak with authority and knowledge. They listen, share information and ensure that there is clarity between them and those who they are leading.

2. Making Decisions

Confident leaders do not second themselves - they make decisions based on the information on hand, their vision and their instinct. If the end result was not the desired outcome - they take responsibility for the decision and the outcome - learn from it - move on.

3. Intelligent Risk Taking

Taking intelligent risks, saying what others dare not say, doing what has never been done before - is one of the signs of a confident leader. Good leaders will courageously take intelligent risks and forge new frontiers - creating opportunities and finding solutions. With each intelligent risk taking the confident leader becomes more and more confident.

4. Optimism

Optimism is the fuel that keeps great leaders focused on the goals for their vision. They know that in spite of challenges, obstacles, hurdles and failures, that showing optimism, backed by a specific action plan. Optimism is what good leadership is all about. It is leadership that empowers.

5. Say no to arrogance

Great leaders know there is a thin line between confidence and arrogance and they err on the side of confidence. People despise those with power who are arrogant. You will fall quickly from the ranks with an attitude of arrogance.

Having confidence is the foundation of great leadership - do you need to build yours today? In the next chapter you will learn how to let people you lead know that you C.A.R.E.

Chapter 8

Let them know you C.A.R.E.

As you endeavor to become the best

leader you can remember to C.A.R.E.

- Count your blessings not your problems
- Actively look for ways to make others a success
- Responsibility for integrity must be your core
- Excellence should be your goal

Always learn all that you can about whatever you do. The moment you as the leader stop growing forward is the moment you stop your dreams. If a doctor were to stop learning about new procedures, new medications or new viruses he becomes antiquated. By not keeping up with the new CDC information he not only jeopardizes his practice but his patients as well. You cannot approach new problems with yesterday's solutions. Take a look at how many phones have changed in your lifetime. Can you imagine trying to do your job walking around with the first model of the cell phone in your pocket? It was so big it wouldn't have fit in your pocket in the first place. Always grow forward as a leader and as a person. Let's look at how using the C.A.R.E. acronym can keep you from derailing you as you push to become a better leader.

> ➤ Count Your Blessings, not your Problems.

Life is full of challenges period. There are so many ups and downs, turns and twists that can sometimes knock the wind right out of you. If you are always looking at the problems that keep popping up, you will become discouraged. When you become discouraged or exhausted then your dreams can get snatched right out from under you.

Here is an important tip to remember when the going gets tough. *Never let a setback make you sit back. Stand up, brush yourself off and make a comeback.*

Don't get so focused on the should haves, would haves, and could haves in your life that you do not see your blessings.

It's like the old "Is the glass half full or half empty" issue. By always seeing that the glass is half empty as a leader you model to those following that whatever you do you cannot get ahead. On the contrary, those that see the glass half full inspire those around them to reach higher and to grow more than they thought they could. Positive leaders up out the best in those that follow them. They see who those around them can be and not what they seem to be at the time.

There is an old hymn found in many church pews across the world. The song says, "Count your blessings name them on by one". Make it a practice to end each day by listing to yourself, with your family, and those you work with to name at least one positive thing that happened. If you do you will not only be more successful but healthier as well. Stress can take a toll on the human body. If you end your day on a positive, then the problems get pushed to the back burner.

> ➢ Actively look for Ways to make Others a Success.

If you are so focused on how you can succeed you will use and abuse those around you. Climbers use people as the stepping stones to their promotions. Great leaders learn how to invest. The most revered leaders in history were not those who rose to the top and made the most money. The greatest leaders are those that encourage, promote, invest, acknowledge and mentor those who follow them. If you want your dream to succeed, then surround yourself with people you know can help grow to get them. If you lead by being self-centered instead of people focused people will read, you like a book. The question must be then what do people see in you? When you leave the room have you made sure everyone knew how important you are. There is a difference between a thermometer and a thermostat. One reads the atmosphere of a room the other sets it. Purpose to be a thermostat and make sure people remember who you are. This leads into the third letter in our acronym

➢ Responsibility for Integrity MUST Be Your Core.

One Sunday school teach had a powerful lesson to her class: Liars are Fryers. Now, she was teaching them an important lesson that a lack of integrity will always bite your behind. You and those around you are at risk when you make promises you can't keep, make yourself be something you're not or live a life with habits that can lead to trouble. If you steal in secret, you can bet someone you are leading will see and do the same.

The word 'Integrity' is defined as *the quality of being honest and having strong moral principles; moral uprightness.*

Synonym Discussion of *integrity* in Miriam Webster's Dictionary states the following;
honesty, honor, integrity, probity mean

uprightness of character or action. honesty implies a refusal to lie, steal, or deceive in any way. Honor suggests an active or anxious regard for the standards of one's profession, calling, or position. integrity implies trustworthiness and incorruptibility to a degree that one is incapable of being false to a trust, responsibility, or pledge. probity implies tried and proven honesty or integrity.

So what kind of example are you leading? Here is a quick tip. What you don't hate you will tolerate. If you don't hate stealing then when you need something you will take it. Even the smallest thing like thinking you need some copy paper for your home office, so you take some from the job. What are you living in front of people? Others are always watching

> Excellence Should Be Your Goal

You must determine to do things right the first time. It's the difference between the functions of a thermostat or a thermometer. A thermostat measures the temperature of its surroundings. A Thermostat sets the temperature of its surrounding. When you walk into a room are you always feeling things out before you move. A great leader can walk into a room and people take notice. There has to be something about you that makes others take notice. You might be asking where you could find that. The answer is only found within you. What makes you unique? Do you exude confidence? Can other see that they can trust you?

To be a good leader you have to practice what you preach. People do not always expect you to be perfect, but to live with integrity and show them how to get back up. What message are you sending? That it's ok just to settle in life or that you can reach for your dreams?

In closing, don't let others dictate to you the kind of leader you should be. Know your leadership skills. Take a good hard look at your strengths and always strive to improve them. Then take a good hard look at your shortcomings and correct them. Being a good leader is an evolutionary process. What you are right now can evolve into the best leader you can imagine. The keys to the vehicle to greatness are in your hands. The closing questions are- what are you going to do? Will you stay in park and settle, or will you drive your way to become a successful leader? Learn all that you can. Lead with integrity and invest in all those around you.

Other great resources to read to help improve your leadership skills.

Top 10 Best Books on Leadership

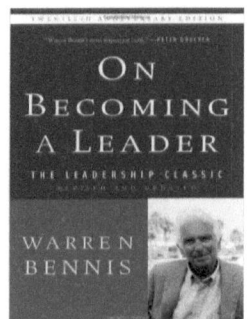

1. On Becoming a Leader **by Warren Bennis (1989)**

Professor Bennis conducts hundereds of interviews with thought leaders to answer the question: What is a good leader? Bennis didn't just limit his interviews to executives (like many leadership books), he included entrepreneurs, psychologists, philosophers, etc… Due to his broad research and definition of leadership, this hits the top of my list.

2. *The Art of War* by Sun Tzu (5th century B.C.)

Who hasn't heard of this book, right? It's amazing to think it was written in 5th century B.C. Many generals, Presidents and CEOs have pulled knowledge from this book over hundreds of years. This book is an Ancient Chinese was manual made up of 13 sections, each highlighting a different aspect of battle strategy. This timeless classic leadership book is full of insights into how not only to set goals but also achieve them. The basic premise is to take action swiftly as a strategy versus making lists. How many of us spend much of our day preparing to prepare? Sun Tzu says "ACT!".

3. *Primal Leadership: Realizing the Power of Emotional Intelligence* by Daniel Goleman (2002)

You may have heard me say, "Vulnerability is the number one quality I look for in a leader." Goleman digs deep on this concept in this leadership book. He applies emotional intelligence to leadership and how we can use our emotions in a positive fashion to lead others. After multiple case studies, he states that leaders with "resonance," the ability to channel emotions in a positive direction, are the most effective and inspiring leaders. This is a very interesting twist to most leadership books and is often overlooked when looking at becoming a great leader.

4. *Drive* by Daniel Pink (2009)

Pink is bringing motivation back into leadership while so many other are focused on leading by fear or through incentives. Now, it may sound a little wishy washy to some of you in the beginning, but as he backs it up with multiple scientific findings, you get drawn in and remember why Zig Ziglar and Jim Rohn are still popular today. This is a refreshing read on an old topic. It brought me back to basics and I hope it does the same for you! Just treat people like people and not assets.

5. *Losing My Virginity: How I Survived, Had Fun, and Made*

a Fortune Doing Business My Way by Richard Branson (2011)
The genius autobiography of one of my favorite heroes! Boy, does Richard Branson know how to make a living ling, right? Ever wonder where he came up with the name "Virgin" for his first business? It was a joke between Branson and his friends about being virgins in this business world. He's created companies all over the world following his own rules for success and with no central headquarters, ensuring no hierarchy and as little bureaucracy as possible. It's an amazing and riveting read for a leadership book or any book, for that matter. He's genius and a great mentor through the written word!

6. *Developing the Leader Within You by John C. Maxwell (2005)*

These principles and practices are available for everyday leaders in every walk of life. It is a lofty calling to lead a group—a family, a church, a nonprofit, a business—and the timeless principles in this book will bring positive change in your life and in the lives of those around you. You will learn the true definition of a leader, the traits of leadership and the difference between leadership and management.

7. Delivering Happiness: A Path to Profits, Passion and Purpose **by Tony Hsieh (2009)**
This fun-loving entrepreneur may be as well-known for his unconventional management principles as he is for his Zappos shoe empire. Tony Hsieh's high-minded manifesto: The workplace can and should be a place where employees find personal fulfillment. To that end, Hsieh focuses on fostering happy, passionate, and communicative staffers. When set against the success story that is Zappos—where there's a free Zappos library, and feel-good training

seminars—it's clear Hsieh is onto something.

8. *Never Give In! The Best of Winston Churchill's Speeches* by Winston S. Churchill (2003)
This collection of speeches are a terrific reminder of Churchill's ability to inspire. Curated by the legendary statesman's grandson, these rousing addresses span Churchill's career from World War I to his honorary induction as a US citizen in 1963—and teem with energy and charisma. Even in the face of grave

uncertainty—an impending Nazi invasion, bombings in London—Churchill exuded resilience and courage. The speeches are also striking in their candidness. He had no speechwriters or spin-doctors.

9. *Wooden on Leadership: How to Create a Winning Organization* by John Wooden (2005)

Easily the most successful college basketball coach in history, 10-time NCAA champion John Wooden was beloved by UCLA players and fans as both a coach and mentor. His

"Pyramid of Success," a triangular diagram illustrating 25 behaviors he saw as critical to personal achievement, is widely cited by management consultants and teambuilders worldwide. Though Wooden authored seven leadership books, this one most pointedly applies to the workplace. Wooden offers both concrete tips—each chapter concludes with a bulleted list of actionable steps—and "big picture" inspiration.

10. *21 Irrefutable Laws of Leadership* by John Maxwell (1998)

Maxwell provides 21 hard-hitting laws of leadership he developed over 30 years of leadership successes and mistakes. He highlights leadership lessons from the worlds of business, sports, religion, politics and military conflict.

I'm sure you can imagine, it was tough to list only 10 books. If you race through these 10, check out Harvard Business Review's list of [leadership books for young leaders](#) which is another great group of books you should consider.

Make life an adventure!

www.ingramcontent.com/pod-product-compliance
Lightning Source LLC
Chambersburg PA
CBHW031446210526
45464CB00005B/2352